NOTES
getting over you
TO YOU

angie n.

Writer's Pocket

First published by Writer's Pocket in 2024

email: publish@writerspocket.com

cover design by Pooja Wadiya

ISBN-13: 978-93-6083-710-5

www.writerspocket.com

To the boy I wrote this on, if you're reading this right now, trust me it was nothing serious but then again, I had to do this because it's not my fault you were really a very good muse.

From the Author

(I strongly suggest reading this section before proceeding with the book. I know it's long and I'm sorry but this gives a proper background story to the roots of this book)

It is frequent for me to hear from others that my synopses do not really provide proper context for my book, and I agree with it. Due to the limited characters I was provided with, I had to condense it in every way possible without eliminating anything important. So, I have dedicated this entire section to just explanations and providing full and raw context to the book. I strongly suggest sparing a few minutes and reading this section before moving forward for the best understanding possible. Thank you.

Walking you through this feels like walking into a labyrinth, since there's so much to it that I could go on and on, so I'm trying to do this in the most condensed way possible. When I said *humble abode* I meant my home, and I wrote these pieces for a certain someone I used to have feelings for.

It is so cliché; I know. But the thing is when people become my muse, I really end up liking my work – which is rare. It is ironic how even my debut book was also on a boy – my first love. However, the similarity between them ends there.

'Notes to you' was written on the eve of New Year 2023 and was done and dusted within 25 days. It was pretty easy completing it since it was nothing but pieces that I wrote on a daily basis. Sometimes, 2 pieces a day, and if my productivity level is good, 5 pieces. I really loved and enjoyed working on it as a project; it was like transferring everything I had bottled up over time into words, and in the most productive way ever.

This book, as you know already, is a compilation of pieces and poetry following a particular theme and written on a particular person like I had mentioned earlier. It was honestly not my best phase or something I take pride in, but you don't choose who you fall for. And that was what happened with me as well. I'm not proud of what happened because the muse of this book isn't someone that I should've fallen for, and I knew it. It was wrong on my end.

Don't get me wrong; it had nothing to do with who he was as a person; it had everything to do with the situation. There was no way it was right harboring feelings for someone who already had someone else, even if he was a sweet guy.

It is kind of funny how I ended up falling because we did not really have long, proper conversations or even hung out that often, but then, it happened. I don't know how, but it did. And to deal with the realization of it all, and the aftermath, I turned to the one thing that keeps me sane and the only way I could cope healthily - *I wrote.* I wrote and wrote and wrote. I wrote so many pieces (some of them did not make it here in the book because I felt like they weren't good enough) until it felt easy to be able to walk away from the situation and him.

And before I could even process what I was doing, I already had so many pieces ready that it would've been illegal and heartless to just leave it there in my phone to rot. So, I converted it into something productive.

Now as I come to the end of this whole explanation part, I want you, as my reader, to note the fact that *I did not write this book for him*. I wrote this book *for* myself, *on* him.

Looking back now, I do not regret falling for him. Instead, I'm grateful no matter how wrong it was because that way, I wouldn't be here, and this book would've never happened.

On the days my feelings were brutal, I wrote pieces that can be considered controversial. However, on the days my feelings were genuine, I wrote things that I truly mean. Some of them may contradict each other so, please note that it was written on different days and moods, so my words depended greatly on the mercy of my feelings.

But, nevertheless, I cannot delineate how grateful I am no matter how wrong it was. I was dealing with severe heartbreak back when I first met him. And because of him, I found it so much easier to not look back - since I had something much more beautiful to look at, in front of me.

I'm glad the truth is finally out of me. The heartache was definitely a bitch but worth it, and as I look back, I do not resent them. Instead, I give them a smile since I now have two completed books at 18. I used them to benefit my career as a writer and now, here it is.

As I finally close this chapter and lock it, I feel content and peaceful. Transferring everything that slowly ate me up into paper really gave me a sense of closure and helped me do what I was so desperate of doing from the very beginning - move on. And as always, not only did writing help me achieve what I had initially loathed myself for - the inability to leave, but also helped in converting all those months into small, simple pieces that collectively joined together to form my second book.

I do not know how worthy they are as poetries or even just as literary pieces, but, even if one of them manages to reach your heart and make you smile, I would like to think I did it, because I write for each and every one of you out there who believes in the power of simple words and who looks for a companion, a friend in the words written by other people, hoping they'd write something that'd speak to you, to your heart and feel less alone. Because I am just like you.

So, this is for you, from just another ordinary girl telling the story of her journey and hoping it speaks to you. From my soul to yours.

I truly hope you like them.

P.S: I initially didn't want to use the word 'love' and even removed it all, because it is a very strong word that holds a lot of power but then again, I did so because it added depth and enhanced the overall quality of the pieces. So please, a reminder to not take every word literally.

Notes to you

Entry 1

~ For you yet never yours

The place is dark; I feel like I'm wilting but my heart still shines with the love I harbour for you. I walk down the similar path of love, all the while bleeding like I always do but for the very first time, it's not the same painful one. Your eyes were what dragged me out of the cage of August. September had never been better. But in October, a piece of me shattered when you turned your back and sealed your lips. I know you were never written in my stars but I thought I could keep you if I never look up because they sealed my reality, but you existed just fine inside my dreams. Taylor mama has never been this right; my scars bled because of your stars yet, this pain brings me comfort and happy tears as they are proof that we met, and I got the chance to shelter fondness for you within me in this lifetime.

I'd take the truth with me to the grave.

Entry 2

I look at you and smile;
Heartbreak has a beautiful face.

Entry 3

~ I'd hold you close in my dreams.

Don't get me wrong. You look beautiful nevertheless. But I like you better in my dreams because there, you are smiling at me. I see you through my cell of guilt and my heart feels full from the sea of beauty that hides so well beneath those brown eyes. Sometimes, I wish I could see you openly out in the broad daylight but then I'm hit with the realization that I'm behind the bars of guilt for a reason. My hands are tied with the cuffs of morals. Yes, I can see you walking down the road with me by your side - the painting is beautiful. The sun is casting a glow on your face. It cannot compete with you; they lose. You make me want to gleam like a kid.

It's true I love being in my dreams more than my reality because we're not impossible there.

Entry 4

On my deathbed, I pray you are the one that I look back on.

Entry 5

They say one day we'd find the reason that would want us to better ourselves. You are mine. With you, I learnt that humans are born selfish. Selflessness is to be implemented, not inborn.

That one dull evening in December, while you are miles away in her arms, I felt an overwhelming sense of selfishness that burnt through my soul because I wanted to be her.

But then, I looked back and saw you smiling down at me, so ever genuinely that something clicked; the buttons changed, sides changed. I changed.

Humans are selfish. I am no different. But I want to feel selfless, be selfless.

For you.

I want to be the one who's happy for you even when it has nothing to do with me. I want to be the one who will smile for you even when I'm burning. I want to be the one who prays for you every chance possible without expecting anything in return.

So, I became that.

And I've never been prouder.

Entry 6

Hope breeds eternal misery. Spencer Hastings from Pretty Little Liars said that. I remember always jumping up and down chanting the said line acting all cool as if I knew what it really meant. Now, as I look at you from a distance to play it safe, my heart breaks more than my hope ever will.

That is the thing. I unconsciously keep hoping even when it continues to break my heart. This was what Spencer truly meant.

Entry 7

I probably would never see you again after March 30th. That is okay.

I'd spend forever reminiscing about you in my writings.

Entry 8

How do I ever say goodbye to you without even meeting you?

To make it easier, I fasten my pace.

Entry 9

I see the English countryside,
Mr. Darcy is approaching Elizabeth in the morning light.
She half-expects him,
He's still all in.
"You have bewitched me. Soul and body," His words.
The link between love and hate finally blurs.

I have always wondered if I'd ever get a face to my Mr. Darcy;
It always had seemed so far.
Now you exist in front of me,
Mr. Darcy, you definitely are.
But I do not accept.
I never will,
Because I am not your Elizabeth.

Entry 10

~ Stranger with flowers

I lean against the wall of love,
It is the only thing that stands pure.
But it is so really tough,
Because it is not the right cure.
Took me so long to find your soul,
It's too late, I am told.
I am aware.
My affection feels nugatory.
All they ever really say is beware;
The dolour of hope fills the story.

Tell me why you and you only,
When it could've been anyone else?
Hurts me like a wicked knife,
That is piercing my heart through hell.

If only you knew how much this hurt.

For heaven's sake, what do I even know about what is happening.
A stranger who happens to pass by your dwelling.
But I do look up to your window and wonder what it's like to be her.

I mean no ulterior motives, no harm.
Just a way to cope with my internal turmoil.
I wish you both nothing but warmth,
I hope heartbreak is what your home avoids.

Entry 11

I know that I cannot have you. But at least I can have the idea of you.

- *will that be sinful as well?*

Entry 12

A new year. That month has gone by.
My soul is still stuck in September anyway. Being stuck has always been like the suffocation of cages. But if being stuck in September is also a cage, I'd throw the key away to the farthest of oceans.

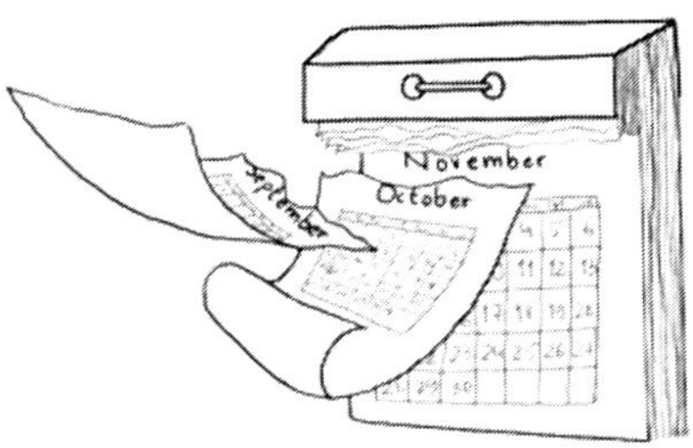

Entry 13

I see you again. It's been a month. But why did it feel like a forever has gone by? You look the same, my friends say. But, they will never understand. You beauty grows tenfold every day.
They say it's my feelings.
Maybe it is, but does it matter? The glow your existence gives to my soul does not seem humanly possible, but here you are. You are looking the other side; I do not exist for you. That is okay.
My scars feel touchable again. I love being in your sunlight.
Thank you for saving me. You'd always be the one I'd write things about.

Entry 14

I will always be fond of the real you.
But I prefer the painting of you better,
Because there, it's fulfilling to want you. Not sinful.

Entry 15

They say history repeats itself. If I were to ever choose which history to repeat, it'd be you.

Entry 16

Walked with me through the road of thorns. Smiled at me when I felt worthless to even get looked at. Lent me a hand and dragged me out before I drowned myself.

And you did it all unconsciously.

Now, I've healed yet I still bleed. I'm off the deep waters yet I'm still drowning. I have crossed the thorny road yet I still feel them under my feet, continuing to draw out blood.

Why?

Because I again fell into a similar deep ocean you previously took me out from, but the one that's in your territory. If only you knew how fulfilling it is to be drowning in yours no matter what they say. If only you knew how I'd much rather die trapped in your ocean than anywhere else.

Simply because I chose to do so.

I thank god every day for giving me a life in the same timeline as you.

Entry 17

My words love you as well. The river flow of my ink has never been this joyful.
A writer's dream is you.

Entry 18

The room lights up when you walk in;
I hold back the urge to walk up and ask you how you've been.
But instead, I look down and sigh.
My friends see my inner turmoil;
They tell me all I can do is avoid.
But, it's been months and I still try.

Ever since September, I've been holding you close.
But in the midst of cherry blossom, I chose to walk away.
I've been trying to do that since October to be very honest with you.
But March was when I could really do it without self-betray.

You're lovely. You always will be. The depth of your softness will always be beyond what humans can embrace. But it's not mine to try.

I hope you knew you were my safe haven.

Entry 19

You will always be my favourite muse.

Entry 20

Every short moment spent with you is worth reminiscing over. I wish you knew how thankful I am for the chance to meet you in this lifetime. It does not matter that at the wrong time because a beautiful soul like yours will always serve as an honour for anybody who crosses path with you. Your smile is the most precious thing I've ever seen, and so for that, if I have to let you go, I accept it.

I'd always embrace the moments I got to look you in the eye and share words and smiles.

Entry 21

I'd forever mourn over just being blessed enough to fall in love with you but never further blessed with the chance to stay in love with you, rather be unfortunate enough to have to let you go because you can never be what I wish you were for me.

Entry 22

I remember you smiling so very beautifully that sunny afternoon, when I shook your hand and congratulated you. Never have I seen you that happy before and I recall wondering how it must be like to be the reason behind bringing one of those smiles to your winsome face.

She gets to be that reason every day. She gets to bring a smile on your face.

Oh to be the luckiest girl living,
Oh to be her.
Because she gets to have you.

Entry 23

The epitome of my starlight is you. One day, I hope from the purest corner of my heart that you'd look back and realize I've felt for you all along.

Until then, I would keep holding on to you from the shadows.

Entry 24

How hard it is to be surrounded by trees of hopelessness. Why do I keep doing this to myself?

I wish I could turn back time and never talked to you. I wish I never looked at you with earphones on that evening because that way, I never would've realized you weren't just a stranger to me. I wish I had never looked too closely to that sheepish smile of yours because that wicked thing can bring someone to their knees.

So many wishes yet, deep down, I know all I truly wish for is to turn back time to when falling for you wouldn't have been such a wrong thing to do. When liking you with every fibre of my being wouldn't have to meet consequences.

Entry 25

If I were to be ever compelled to tell you about my true feelings, I'd rather face the consequences of not doing so because it's better to live in the painful fantasy of mine than to meet with the face of uncertainties that may forever alter the fantasy.

Entry 26

If I were to be Elizabeth, I'd wish for you as my Mr. Darcy.
If I were to be Josephine, I'd wish *for* you to be my Mr. Bhaer.
If I were to be Emma, I'd wish for you to be my Mr. Knightley.

But I'm not. I don't get to be them. It's not a story that was written by Austen or Alcott. It's a story written by reality. And in this story, having you just as an acquaintance is something I've been expected to be fine with. I have to, for the betterment of all. I do not get to be selfish, and most certainly, I do not wish to be selfish.

However, by prospect of any means, if I get to chance to love you again in another lifetime, I hope from the deepest depths of my wretched heart that you'd be right there - the exact same place where my heart chose to walk away from.

I hope you'd be right there, glowing as ever, as beautiful as my heart has always found you, finally unengaged and possible to be cherished the way my heart has always longed to.

Entry 27

God really had favourites.
Look at you.

Entry 28

You feel like *reading* my favourite book.

Entry 29

How funny is it that I think of you when I read romances because it's almost as if I'm trying to manifest you.
Oh, I would've if only my conscience lets me cross the bridge.
Sometimes, I feel the urge to just do it but then, my conscience shows me how truly dark the other side is, how if one crosses the bridge to the other side, one would forever be doomed with darkness and iniquity.
My eyes are then opened.
As much as I adore you, I'd much rather stay this side and cherish you from afar. My heart will be broken but at least, my goodness will stay intact.

I promise to forever root for your happiness.

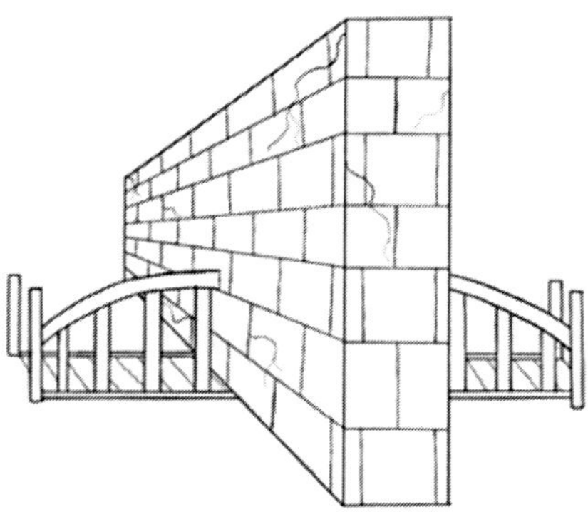

Entry 30

I'm always surrounded by absolute light and pure beauty. But, you are the only one that glow and stand out to me.

Entry 31

The dolour of August was like a world with no light. I wandered around like a blind person, the tears stinging my eyes and calling out for anybody. I could not even wipe my own tears as I continued to drag myself through the utter darkness.

Just then, a slight breeze blew in my direction. Unbeknownst to me, it carried the whisper of a beautiful change that was about to take place. Almost immediately, the season changed. I started seeing cherry blossoms everywhere. My tears were then replaced with smiles. The wind blew lovingly as if I graced them with my presence. I had never felt this pleasant and calm before.

The new season was you.

Entry 32

And suddenly, all of *my* dreams felt incomplete because you wouldn't be in the picture.
I am fucked; in the most fulfilling way.

Entry 33

One day I'd look back and you will be just a memory. A guy who I once felt for. I would sigh finally feeling nothing when I think of you. The cold breeze wouldn't sting anymore, wouldn't mock anymore. I would walk down the road with just memories and not feelings.

On days it broke my heart to feel for you, I wanted nothing but this. But truly and deeply, I don't want that day to come, because I don't want to be someone who doesn't get butterflies when they see you.

I don't ever want to become someone who harbours nothing for you.

Entry 34

I’ve always found rain and cherry blossoms the prettiest of all.
You beat them.

Entry 35

September was our month. You'd always be that boy to me that I met then. October, the chain of hope that you tied onto me broke loose in a swift painful motion. But, ironically, it was also the month I fell in love with you. No matter how it turned out, I promise to always remember you as the boy who waved at me that September evening telling me how you started reading the school newsletter again.

Entry 36

Taylor mamma said, *"My thoughts will echo your name until I see you again."* Except that I do not know for sure if I'll ever see you again. They say the world is small but not small enough for you to not get lost in the noisy crowd with no face. Why does it feel like your hand is slipping away from me even though I never held it in the first place? The night is pitch dark and the ruthless wind seems to be mocking me. I let out a breath that creates a fog in this cold. I'm not surprised there is no moon. How can there be when you are nowhere to be seen?

Entry 37

Oh to be so lucky that one gets to cross paths with you in this busy lifetime.
It always enchants me that I'm one of them.

Entry 38

With time, these feelings will fade.
This old skin of mine will shed.
I'd move on too, carrying nothing but your memories.
I'd walk away someday, with everything about you that I'll miss.
But, it's for the best; this is how it works.
What a beautiful mess - I like it here even though it hurts.

Some days, I sense it beginning to fade,
That I'm no longer in love.
Though I don't want to ever remember the date,
Because I never want to be someone for whom you aren't enough.

Entry 39

I sit here,
Writing the last piece.
The door away from you looks near.
I'm supposed to have happy dreams.
I found a reason to walk away,
Though one might find it queer.
It seems the ending wouldn't be cliché.
The finished artwork of you wasn't what I thought it was.

However, still, I feel blessed enough to have gotten the chance to carry fondness in heart for you.

Still, very much this stands true.

But, this reason, I cannot really get through.

It hurts, but I got to do what I got to do.

Do not worry, though; I won't regret having you for my second *book.*

Someone who is blooming in the garden of gratitude you planted

ABOUT THE AUTHOR

Angie N is a 19 year old writer, currently pursuing her first year as a UG student. She has been a writer ever since she could spell her name but, she started giving herself the title when she started writing her debut book when she was 15. It was self-published last year in October, 2022. A Taylor Swift worshipper, she believes in the supremacy of her music, sad songs and The Wizard Liz. This is her second book and the result of the numerous nights and days she spent, trying to pull herself out of the labyrinth of vulnerability and hurt, converted into ink and put together by many single pages that eventually became a book.

Acknowledgement

Y'all, can you believe this is my second book????? Like, at 18, I have two completed books??? And at 19, both are out??? AHHH THANK YOU THANK YOU THANK YOU FOR CHOOSING TO READ MY WORK WHEN YOU COULD'VE CHOSEN ANYTHING ELSE. I'm beamingwith gratitude *cries* you don't know this so let me tell you that you're contributing HUGE TIME into making my 8 year old self proud. So thank you so much!<3

Firstly, to my folks, thank you so so SO much for believing in my dreams so much more than anything else, and supporting me 24/7 into becoming someone I want to be. Your faith restores my confidence every single time I doubt.

To my brother, I hope you're proud to call me your sister.

To Gengam, a dear friend AND also roommate from senior year, thank you for the illustrations<3 your efforts during the last few months before I submitted the book made it possible.

Grandpa, I miss you everyday and forever. I hope you are resting in peace and finally happy. I love you so much.

Oja Chingkhei, there will never be a time I write something and don't mention you in my acknowledgement. From a confused, rebellious 9th grader who thought life wasn't worth it, to the girl who now looks at herself and feels proud, you did it all.

To my cute dadou and both of my bobok, thank you for all the love over the years. To my entire family from both sides, nene and kakas, I hope you're proud of me. This is a small gift for all the love y'all have showered me with over the years.

To my sweetest Hana, you think you didn't do much to make it here but trust me, all those little things you do for me with utmost dedication and honesty as if it means as much to you as it does to me makes you so worthy to be a part of this. So, keep glowing boss lady. Thank you will never be enough to show you how thankful I am to have you in my life. So much love for you always <333

To my cousins: Linthoi, Naopik, Abemma, Che Princy, Che Mu. I literally cannot, CANNOT form enough words to appreciate y'all for every single time I confided in you and I never felt let down. ILY.

Jaskee Paaji, keeping my promise to you one book at a time <3

Sammy, you held my hand during one of my worst moments and you've not dropped it ever since. To find someone like you is everybody's dream, and I got you. Promise I'll always have your back.

To my friends: Adie, Riia, Claudi, Sarai, Priya, Harshi, Mahita, Migam, Prat, Adella, Tem. Thank you for all those 3 hours long lectures. I still learnt nothing :D

To my college buddies: Anurag (Stripper), Yang, Mono, Adrija, Shivangi, Rebecca. LY SM.

To my mamma mia:) thank you for always having my back.

Don Don, I don't need words for you because you will continue to always rock for me. I miss you so much please come back soon to the country and stop being so subtly shady towards me all the time lol.

KHRIESI, got to thank you on this one. You know why cupid ;)

Dush, this one is for always hyping me like no other.

To the uncles I never got to bid a goodbye, I know we were never close but thank you for all those moments you treated me like your own.

To the one who knows exactly who he is, the pieces that you so adore are now finally out as we had always talked about. I hope you still like them. Thank you for everything (especially for the great escape. Ykwim). You were my roman empire for a really long while.

And lastly but not the least, a HUGE thank you to my publishers. Thank you for working with me on this.